I lift mine eyes unto the hills.

From whence doth come mine aid. . . .

—PSALM 121

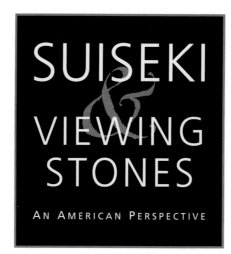

SUISEKI
&
VIEWING
STONES

AN AMERICAN PERSPECTIVE

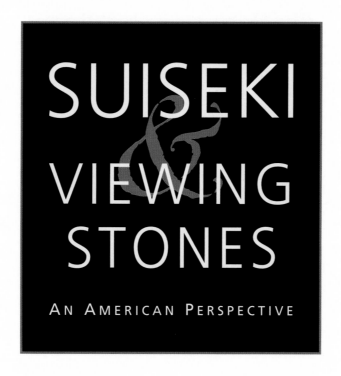

SUISEKI & VIEWING STONES

AN AMERICAN PERSPECTIVE

Melba L. Tucker

PHOTOGRAPHY BY **Peter L. Bloomer**

EDITED BY **Mary Holmes Bloomer and Peter L. Bloomer**

Horizons West
FLAGSTAFF, ARIZONA

To my husband, Ned Tucker, who for many years helped me water and repot bonsai, search for suiseki and viewing stones, and make dais for many of my stones, and who encouraged and supported me in my hobby.

To my son, Ronald T. Tucker, 1947–1988.

To my daughter, Mariana Lee Walsh, who has supported me in many ways. She has unselfishly requested that my suiseki, "Geisha Girl," when I am no longer here to care for it, not go into one person's collection, but rather be placed where many people can enjoy this beautiful piece of art created by nature.

■   ■   ■

Text copyright © 1996 by Melba L. Tucker

Photographs © 1996 by Peter L. Bloomer unless otherwise noted. All rights reserved.

Published by Horizons West, Flagstaff, Arizona

Distributed by Stone Lantern Publishing Co.
P.O. Box 816, Sudbury, MA 01776
Phone 978/443-7110   FAX 978/443-9115
order@stonelantern.com

Book design by Larry Lindahl Design

Calligraphy by John Fortune

Display and text type set in Frutiger Roman and Bold

Printed by South Sea International Ltd.

ISBN 0-9634423-2-5

Library of Congress Cataloging-in-Publication Data

Tucker, Melba L.
Suiseki and viewing stones : an American perspective / by Melba L. Tucker ; photography by Peter L. Bloomer ; edited by Mary Holmes Bloomer and Peter Bloomer.
  p.   cm.
ISBN 0-9634423-2-5
1. Suiseki. 2. Bonsai. I. Bloomer, Mary Holmes, 1941- . II. Bloomer, Peter L., 1940- .
III. Title.
NK8715.T83 1996
745.58'4—dc20   96-4932

Acknowledgments

There are many people I would like to acknowledge, not only for their help and support in putting this book together, but also for their knowledge, friendship, and expertise during my development in and appreciation of suiseki over many years. Most recently, without the special efforts of Peter and Mary Bloomer in photography and editing, this publication would not have been possible. Encouragement from Tom and Sena Zane, along with their tireless efforts, got the project started. The special interest and work of Marge Blasingame and Dien Liang kept me going forward. Thanks also go to Harry Hirao for generously allowing me to include his stone in this book.

I would also like to thank my many, many friends who donated to the National Bonsai and Penjing Museum in Washington, D.C., so that the Suiseki Display Area might be named in my honor. I am gratified and humbled and proud of the privilege of having so many friends.

Author's Preface

The purpose of this book is to share with you my joy in collecting suiseki and viewing stones.

While creating living landscapes (saikei) with bonsai trees and rocks, I became interested in the rocks themselves. The different forms, shapes, and textures intrigued me. Around 1971, through my contacts with the late Don Sanborn, I was introduced to suiseki and viewing stones, and I began acquiring them. Mr. Sanborn lived in Japan, and he came to the United States and attended many bonsai conventions and exhibits. All of the stones that he showed and sold were imported from Japan. I bought some, but soon learned that I too could collect them from nature—in America.

I went on many collecting trips with Tony Thomas, Bob Watson, and Cliff Johnson.

Most of the stones that I personally collected were found on these outings into the Mojave Desert and to the rivers, lakes, and mountains of California. It was on one of these trips into the Mojave that I found my "Geisha Girl," the pride of my collection, which graces the cover of this book and is described on page 7.

During these collecting trips into the Mojave Desert, I'd come to realize that Americans have some unique and beautiful types of stones that do not fit into any previously known classification scheme. Over a period of time we have developed our own unique ways of looking at stones, based on the images and experience of our own landscapes. This prompted my wish to share the art of suiseki and viewing stones as seen from an American's perspective.

The classical art of suiseki and viewing stones originated in the Far East, as did the art of bonsai. As these art forms were being accepted and practiced in the Western world, they evolved and underwent changes. Bonsai, primarily an Eastern art form, is now practiced by Americans with American trees. So too can suiseki and viewing stones be collected in America by Americans. Many of the suiseki and viewing stones found in this country are different from those that have been collected over the years in the Far East. They are different, but their difference makes them of no less interest or value to those who appreciate the art.

The title of this book is *Suiseki and Viewing Stones: An American Perspective.*

What I mean by "an American perspective" of stone appreciation is an adaptation of the classical concepts developed in the Far East. These classical concepts are outlined in the book *The Japanese Art of Stone Appreciation,* by Vincent T. Covello and Yuji Yoshimura. Once we learn the principles behind these concepts and why they were developed, then we are free to adapt them for our enjoyment and pleasure. If an American collector of suiseki and viewing stones likes a particular stone that doesn't seem to fit into one of the historical classifications, he may develop his own classification, rooted in the established principles but based on an American experience. He is free to enjoy his art in the American way.

Suiseki and Viewing Stones

An American Perspective

Bringing new information to the discussion of an ancient art is not my goal. What I hope to do is simply present what suiseki has come to mean to me and what it has brought to my appreciation of the art form. Nothing here is meant to contradict others and their definitions or viewpoints, only, I hope, to add to the ever-expanding appreciation of beautiful stones.

The word *suiseki* can be used to describe the art form or to describe a stone that fits into the art. It is generally agreed that the word translates from the Japanese as "water stone." The term probably originates from the likelihood that the best, earliest collected stones were found in rivers where water (and waterborne abrasives such as sand) had formed their shape. Most prized stones from those early days of stone appreciation depicted mountains, terrain with plateaus or multilevel steps, islands with bay inlets, or landscapes with waterfalls or streams. According to most collectors with an acknowledged expertise in this art form, an individual suiseki should also have the physical qualities of being a smooth, hard stone, usually black or at least dark in color, and preferably unaltered from the form in which it was found. A glance through any publication showing a collection of stones, however, quickly reveals that many highly prized pieces go beyond that narrow definition.

A stone viewed for its own beauty, for the image it conjures in the mind of the viewer, fits somewhere in the universe of the art form. Today, the art has come to include a much wider variety of shapes, images, and fantasies. Because these stones were created by nature, shaped by nature, unaltered by human hands, and yet can be understood universally for what they depict, they offer something special—a spiritual feeling when viewed.

Desert stones found in the southwestern United States have very different geologic origins than "traditional" stones. Metamorphosed mud, limestone with chert (a type of quartz), volcanics, very hard sandstones, and mixtures of these with colors created by the presence of iron, copper, magnesium, and sulfur all yield a variety of material that has become prized by a growing number of collectors. A sense of awe draws me to these exquisite stones as I realize the millions of years in their creation and the beauty and variety of the shapes I see when I find and display them.

For me, the narrow definition above is a starting point. Some of our desert stones fit very well into the scope that defined early suiseki. Others have different colors, shapes, or degrees of smoothness. A criteria I use is size. While it is generally accepted that one's ability to hold the stone in one's hand (or hands) defines a size limit, my hands are smaller and my strength less, so I have come to appreciate smaller stones. As you read about the illustrated stones, I may refer to some stones I can most comfortably hold as suiseki. Others I may refer to as viewing stones. This does not infer that the terms used by others are wrong or that I am right, it is simply a part of this American perspective. Imagine, if you will, finding a stone you felt had exquisite characteristics but did not fit some defined criteria for suiseki. How unhappy you would be later as you lamented leaving it behind based on what you've been led to believe defines suiseki.

One category of stones that falls into another realm includes those that have been polished or reshaped to enhance colors or images within the stone. These are called *biseki*. *Biseki* means "beautiful stone" and opens a little wider the world of stone appreciation.

An art form related to the beauty of natural stones was first developed in China during the thirteenth century. From there this art migrated to Korea, then Japan, during the fourteenth century. At first only members of the nobility could afford this expression of Zen.

Centuries later, as happened with much Oriental art, suiseki found acceptance in England, and then North America, where it was especially welcomed by bonsai enthusiasts in the United States and Canada. Now collectors throughout Europe and the world are bringing an appreciative eye to fine stones.

It is no surprise that interest in and desire for suiseki often accompanies a love of bonsai. After caring for bonsai for many years, a person naturally develops an eye for these representations of nature in miniature. Trees and rocks are natural partners. The glory of finding the perfect suiseki is a thrill. The collector instantly obtains a piece of art that will live forever. Unlike bonsai, it doesn't need any special care. It's just there to be enjoyed. Both bonsai and suiseki can provide a real joy in one's life.

The classification of suiseki was developed by the Japanese, as were the rules pertaining to the art of bonsai. Shape, proportions, and the projected image or pattern all were given names. As these found sufficient repetition, they became specific classifications. The stones illustrated here are shown with their Japanese classification, preceded by the English translation. Additionally, an appendix includes a listing of the major classical categories.

Presentation of any art form is important. It is no different for stones, which can be "framed" to show at their best. There are two common approaches to suiseki display. Perhaps the most widely used is the *dai,* a stand specially made for the particular stone. Hardwood, left natural or stained black or various shades of brown, is the preferred material.

In constructing a dai it is important that it complement the shape, color, texture, and scale of the stone. The points of visual weight around the perimeter of the stone should be where the dai's feet are placed, keeping them in proportion to the stone and to the dai itself. The outline of the base of the stone must be carved into the dai so that the stone fits securely, following the edge closely. There are various techniques in designing and carving these dai, but they are beyond the scope of this book. A recent development is the use of a product called Bondo, a commercially available, synthetic material used most frequently in auto body repair. It has the advantage of being able to be molded to the shape of the stone, and it is weatherproof, so that stones can be displayed outside where wood might be damaged. Use of this material is a specialized technique that should not be attempted without instruction.

The question of fitting the stone into a dai raises the issue of whether or not flattening the bottom by cutting the stone before framing is acceptable. There is no absolute answer. Some believe it is inappropriate and reduces the value of the stone. Others feel it is not only acceptable, but desirable, enhancing the value. Value is a relative term. Altering the natural shape or appearance of a stone may decrease its intrinsic value but increase its aesthetic value. It probably depends largely on the stone itself, and it is perhaps best to let each collector make his or her own decision in this matter.

The other most commonly used method of display is placing the stone in a *suiban.* A suiban is a shallow container, without holes in the bottom, usually of kiln-fired clay. Colors vary from gray, green, white, and various shades of blue to the unglazed brown so typical in bonsai pots. Color should be selected to complement the stone. Shapes cover the range of round to oval, square to rectangular. To avoid having the suiban visually dominate the stone, it is necessary that it be very shallow, with no lip, and in a proportion appropriate to the stone. Sand is used in the suiban to give the illusion of water or ground, an illusion that can be enhanced by the color and texture of the sand. Off-white to various shades of light brown are most commonly used. Aesthetically, it is important to have the sand smoothed around the stone for a clean, "untrampled" look. A feather, or small brush, or any number of other techniques can be used to smooth the sand.

Water can also be used in the suiban, with the obvious reference to the sea or a lake. A blue glazed suiban is a good choice for this sort of display. For example, a shelter stone of the proper color can be placed in a blue suiban with water. Adding a small figure under the shelter and a small boat out in the water creates an entire scene of peace and tranquility. More than one or two objects would begin to distract from the stone, but experimentation develops your sense of what you like and what works.

With either sand or water, placement of the stone to the left or right within the suiban makes for a dynamic display, while centering is more static and generally less pleasing. The visual movement of the stone should determine the left or right placement. If you wish to use a stand to complete your display, it is very important to select one that complements rather than distracts. This is true whether the stone is displayed in a dai or a suiban. Often, no stand is needed, particularly when the stone has a dai. But for a small stone in a dai or a stone in a suiban, a simple table, stand, or wood slab is appropriate, and can give height to the display. This is an area where the collector of suiseki and viewing stones can put his or her own artistic feeling into showing off a prized piece.

Recently, as suiseki has grown in popularity, a new method of display has been used at shows in Southern California. A fine stone might be accompanied by a small accent piece such as grass or other small plants, even flowering or fruiting bonsai. With the stone as the larger of the two, and the display completed on a very simple stand or flat piece of natural wood, a great deal of interest and variety is added to a show.

Given the origins of suiseki appreciation in China, the display of stones most commonly seen there is also gaining popularity here. Using a shallow white marble tray, stones are assembled in groups to resemble a landscape. This gives a different dimension to the art.

As bonsai in America has matured to appreciate American trees and American styles, so too is suiseki in the U.S. evolving to this point. No matter where the stone was found, the experience of the American landscape provides a unique perspective. Each stone evokes a response based on the viewer's experience. My experience is that of the desert Southwest, and most of my stones are from that area. This is the world of suiseki I wish to share with people everywhere, whether they have been to the desert or would like to go there someday.

Double-peaked mountain stone *(Soho-seki)*
1" tall and 2" wide
California desert

This is a very small suiseki depicting two mountain peaks. The dai was carved by Gail Middleton.

"Geisha Girl"
Pattern stone *(Mon'yo-seki)*
(Human-pattern stone)
8¹/₂" tall and 8" wide
Mojave Desert, California

This is a very special example of a type of stone found in the California desert. Known as "Indian Blanket stone" because of its varied colors and patterns, it opens up a new world to the imagination. To get to the area where this suiseki was collected, it was necessary to use a dune buggy and go into the desert eight miles from the highway. I first saw a fairly obvious scene of a tree on a mountain slope in the pattern. Some time later an older Japanese gentleman exclaimed to me, "I see the silhouette of a geisha girl." Since that time, she is what I see, and that is the name I have chosen for the stone. This is a prime example of the viewer having the choice of what to see. The dai was carved by my husband, Ned.

Distant mountain stone *(Toyama-ishi)*
1¹/₂" tall and 2¹/₂" wide
California

This is a treasure to me. It is a prize suiseki when viewed from either side and is set off by the appearance of fog at the base of the mountain. It was displayed at one of the first suiseki shows in Southern California, at the Huntington Gardens in San Marino. There, an elderly Japanese gentleman, a known suiseki expert, judged it as best in show.

These two biseki have been enhanced by being slightly polished (but not carved). The one on the right is an exquisite blending of color, white to cream, tan to rust, and gray to blue, yielding a beautiful abstract pattern.

On the left is an Indian Blanket stone with an abstract leaf pattern of three leaves on the front and one on the back. The "polishing" of these stones was mainly nature's handiwork. In one case, the stone was tumble-polished in a river for tens of thousands of years. In the other, wind-driven sand has done the work.

Beautiful stone *(Biseki)*
5 1/2" tall and 6" wide
Eel River, California

Leaf-pattern stone *(Hagata-ishi)*
6" tall and 5 1/2" wide
California desert

Animal-shaped stone *(Dobutsu-seki)*
2" tall and 3 1/2 " wide
California desert

This suiseki needs no explanation. He's my
Scottish terrier saying, "How could you help
but like me? I'm proud to be one of a kind."

Human-shaped stone *(Sugata-ishi)*
3" tall and 3 1/2 " wide
Mojave Desert, California

This is a different and interesting
suiseki because it has two "views."
From the side shown, it appears to
be a man pushing an overloaded
wheelbarrow. From the other side,
it becomes a dog (Dobutsu-seki)
with a bushy tail and a puppy
behind her feet.

Distant mountain stone *(Toyama-ishi)*
2" tall and 5" wide
California river

The rounded profile of this smooth black suiseki projects the image of a distant mountain. Its display, in an unglazed brown suiban with the mountain peak one-third the distance from the left edge, accents the vision of a mountain across the vast plain.

Waterfall stone *(Taki-ishi)*
2" tall and 3" wide
California desert

A striking white quartz waterfall defines this mountain of hard, dark and light gray stone. These features, plus its small size, make it very desirable as a suiseki.

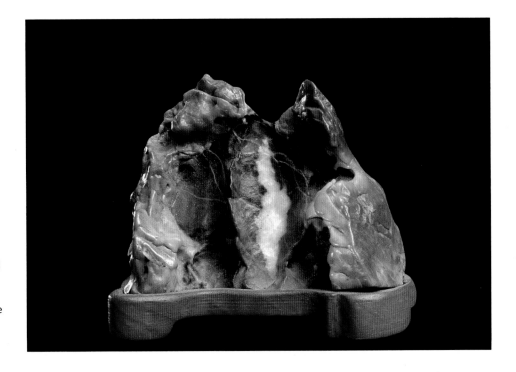

Near-view mountain stone *(Kinzan-seki)*
1¹/₂" tall and 4" wide
South Africa

In this stone's rugged features, sloping shoulders, and interesting colors (from grays to reddish brown) one can easily sense the proximity of a nearby mountain range. The dai was carved by Ned Tucker.

Plateau or step stone *(Dan-ishi)*
1" tall and 3" wide
South Africa

Smooth and dark brown, this is a nearly perfect suiseki. It has three plateaus in good proportion to one another. The top step is one-half the length of the second step. The third step is two times the length of the second step. A favorite, it was a gift to me from a collector in South Africa.

Plateau stone *(Dan-ishi)*
1" tall and 3" wide
South Africa

Three distinct plateaus, the lowest running full length, the middle one two inches long, and the highest one an inch long, evoke an ancient landscape. This is a very small, smooth, dark brown suiseki that I was fortunate to collect in South Africa.

Shelter stone *(Yadori-ishi)*
2" tall and 4 1/2" wide
Indonesia

Two overhanging shelters define this hard, dark brown suiseki, appropriately displayed in a suiban. This stone was a gift from Fritz vander Kruijf of the Netherlands, and is an example of how the art of suiseki helps unite people from all over the world, bringing us a little closer together.

Scenic landscape stone *(Sansui kei-seki)*
4 1/2" tall and 8" wide
Mojave Desert, California

Though it doesn't distinctly fit into one of the previously established subcatagories of landscape stones, this rugged piece with its deep canyon and honey-colored tones typifies the landscape of the American southwestern desert.

Waterfall stone *(Taki-ishi)*
8" tall and I5" wide
Lake Hill, California

Collected in 1974, long before Lake Hill became part of a national reserve, this stone has a smooth, hard, black surface with quartz forming several waterfalls. It has not been cut or altered in any way. Cliff Johnson carved the dai to flow with and fit the shape of the stone, perfectly complementing its beauty. It can be seen in Washington, D.C., at the National Bonsai and Penjing Museum's Melba L. Tucker Suiseki Display Area.

These two object stones represent birds. The one on the left is a hard, smooth sandstone. It is displayed on a thicker wood dai, which is necessary for balance. The one on the right—a mother hen sitting on eggs—is a hard, smooth, black suiseki.

Bird-shaped stone *(Torigata-ishi)*
6" tall and 2¹/₂" wide
Indio, California

Bird-shaped stone *(Torigata-ishi)*
3" tall and 4" wide
California desert

Animal-shaped stone *(Dobutsu-seki)*
2" tall and 3¹/₂" wide
California desert

This fearsome fellow is made up of gray-blue Paleozoic limestone and honey-colored chert (quartz). See his gaping mouth? When his head is tipped back, his teeth are visible. Doesn't he look like a dinosaur straight out of *Jurassic Park*?

Bird-shaped stone *(Torigata-ishi)*
4" tall and 4" wide
California desert

Perched on a rocky ledge, this bird is sitting on her nest. The suiseki is black, with light and dark gray Paleozoic limestone, carved and polished by wind and blowing sand.

Object stone *(Keisho-seki)*
3" tall and 2" wide
California desert

Object stone *(Keisho-seki)*
2¹/₂" tall and 2¹/₂" wide
California desert

Object stone *(Keisho-seki)*
3" tall and 2" wide
California desert

Here are four small stones with visual variety: on the top left, a leaning tower; next, a stone with a storm cloud and a bolt of lightning streaking down a column of rain; third, a mushroom; and bottom left, an Indian Blanket stone with the pattern of a large leaf across the lower portion.

Leaf-pattern stone *(Hagata-ishi)*
4" tall and 2" wide
California desert

Photo by Marge Blasingame

Near-view mountain stone *(Kinzan-seki)*
8" tall and 9" wide
Lake Hill, California

A viewing stone that could be called "Teton Peaks" after the famous mountains of Jackson Hole, Wyoming, this has a smooth, very hard, black surface. The three peaks and three patches of snow give one the view of the mountains from the valley floor. Note how the feet of the dai have been placed under the parts of the stone with the heaviest visual weight.

Object stone *(Keisho-seki)*
(Bonsai tree)
2 1/2" tall and 1 3/4" wide
Mojave Desert, California

A tree that will live for all eternity, this rare and unusual suiseki is a perfect representation of a bonsai tree. The chert layers in the stone are the tree's foliage. It can be viewed equally well from either side, so its "front" is debatable. Its display is enhanced by the dai, carved to look like a display table under the tree, ready for a show. The dai was carved by Gail Middleton.

Waterfall stone *(Taki-ishi)*
2 1/2" tall and 5" wide
California desert

Cascading down this hard, black stone is a white quartz waterfall. The waterfall starts at the very top, hidden at its source by mountain peaks, and bursts down just one side of the stone. Divided by a boulder in midstream, this torrent sweeps everything in its path.

Coastal rock stone *(Iwagata-ishi)*
3" tall and 4¹/₂" wide
California river

The rugged coastal rock surrounded
by rough waters indicated the
classification for this suiseki.
Hard, black stone fused by
nature to the white quartz
makes it unusual and special.

Photo by Marge Blasingame

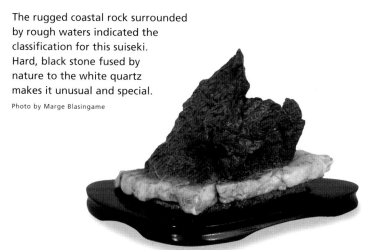

Near-view mountain stone *(Kinzan-seki)*
8" tall and 11" wide
Mojave Desert, California

Jagged peaks and steep cliffs with white patches that
look like snow accentuate the sense of the closeness
of this mountain range. As an example of how people
see things differently, three men with whom I was
collecting picked up and discarded this stone, while I
was glad to give it a happy home.   Photo by Marge Blasingame

Bird-shaped stone *(Torigata-ishi)*
9" tall and 11" wide
Lake Hill, California

An excellent example of how one can see different
things in viewing stones, this stone can be seen as
two duck heads, therefore "Torigata-ishi," or as a
twin or double-peaked mountain stone, "Soho-seki."
It is uncut and unaltered from the way it was found.

Shelter stone *(Yadori-ishi)*
4" tall and 11" wide
Indio, California

Two distinct "shelters," one twice as long as the other, and a long profile invite
us in from the elements as we view this suiseki. It is very hard sandstone, giving
it the quality needed to be classed as suiseki.

Island stone *(Shimagata-ishi)*
1" tall and 5" wide
Indio, California

This island, with its deep cove and low profile, could also be displayed in a suiban, with off-white sand depicting the water.

Distant mountain stone *(Toyama-ishi)*
4¹/₂" tall and 10" wide
Russian River, California

This is an excellent suiseki, with its dark jade green color and a surface worn smooth by the constant flow of water.

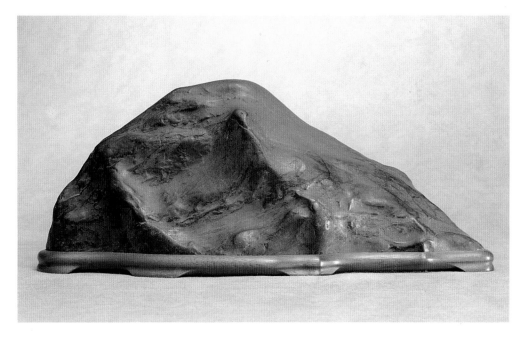

Two examples of stones that have been polished to accentuate the pattern of the flowers so prized by the Japanese, these suiseki were collected in Japan. Because they have been polished, some collectors would, arguably, consider these stones to be biseki (beautiful stones) rather than suiseki.

Chrysanthemum-pattern stone *(Kikumon-seki)*
2¹/₂" tall and 3¹/₂" wide
Japan

Chrysanthemum-pattern stone *(Kikumon-seki)*
3¹/₂" tall and 4" wide
Japan

String-pattern or
Tangled-net-pattern stone *(Itomaki-ishi)*
3" tall and 3" wide
Arizona

White veins of quartz give the impression of
a ball of string or a tangled net.

Abstract-pattern stone *(Chusho-seki)*
5" tall and 7" wide
California river

The white circles form an unusual design in this
polished black biseki. It would be better displayed
in a wider, shorter dai.

Object stone *(Keisho-seki)*
12" tall and 13" wide
Wyoming river

This stone is sensational for its sensuous lines and jet-black, satiny surface. It defies classification by shape or pattern, for each who views it will see something different in it. Collected in a river in Wyoming by Kunika Nakawatase, it is unaltered in any way. This magnificent viewing stone was a gift to Harry Hirao (pictured above) and is the only one in this book that has not been in the author's personal collection. The unusual but perfectly complementary dai was carved by George Konishi.

Coastal rock stone *(Iwagata-ishi)*
6" tall and 8" wide
Indio, California

Ocean waves have undercut the face of this dark pink, hard, semi-smooth sandstone. It has not been altered in any way. Cliff Johnson carved the dai.

Beautiful stone *(Biseki)*
10" tall and 14" wide
California desert

Not strictly a suiseki, this is an excellent specimen of Indian Blanket stone. I think you can see the reason for this name as the patterns of red, brown, beige, and white look much like the blankets and rugs woven by Native Americans. The stone has been polished to bring out the beauty of its colors, but it has not been lacquered or altered in any other way. Cliff Johnson polished the stone and carved its dai.

Human-shaped stone *(Sugata-ishi)*
5" tall and 1¹/₂" wide
California desert

Human-shaped stone *(Sugata-ishi)*
4¹/₂" tall and 1¹/₂" wide
California desert   Photo by Marge Blasingame

Human-shaped stone *(Sugata-ishi)*
4¹/₂" tall and 2" wide
California desert

These three examples of object stones with a human shape add much humor to the art of suiseki. The lady on the left is clearly a Californian saying, "I'm so tall that every time there's an earthquake I fall, but do you like my hat?" The little fellow in the middle looks for all the world like someone from out of this world. His perfect little turned-up feet make him a bit unsteady. He was collected by my husband Ned. The third stone is a Peruvian Indian wearing a hat and shawl to keep him warm in the mountain winds.

Animal-shaped stone *(Dobutsu-seki)*
2" tall and 3" wide
California desert

Animal-shaped stone *(Dobutsu-seki)*
3¹/₂" tall and 4¹/₂" wide
California desert

Animal-shaped stone *(Dobutsu-seki)*
2¹/₂" tall and 6" wide
California desert

These three object stones are examples of seeing animals represented in suiseki. Sometimes the animal is seen in the stone's shape, sometimes in the pattern embedded in the stone. Above left, we have an anteater. The desert frog (left) is well camouflaged, but I spotted him anyway. Can you see his two eyes? The alligator (above right) is sunning himself on a rock . . . waiting for dinner to come by, perhaps?

Plateau stone *(Dan-ishi)*
3" tall and 10" wide
California desert

This suiseki was found in 1976 by Bob Watson, who introduced me to the beauties of Indian Blanket stones. The sometimes subtle, sometimes sharply contrasting shades of red, black, and beige set off the plateau shape of the stone. I subsequently purchased the stone from Bob, and later donated it to the National Bonsai and Penjing Museum.

Plateau stone *(Dan-ishi)*
4" tall and 9" wide
Northern California river

A fine, smooth, black suiseki with three plateaus, this stone was a gift to me from Ernie Kuo. It is displayed in a suiban eighteen inches wide with light-colored sand.

Island stone *(Shimagata-ishi)*
1¹/₂" tall and 5" wide
California

This "island" has two mountain peaks and a beautiful, sheltering cove. An excellent stone, it could be displayed in a suiban with water or, as here, in its dai, placed on a lacquered wood stand to reflect its image as water would. The dai was carved by Gail Middleton.

Shelter stone *(Yadori-ishi)*
3¹/₂" tall and 4¹/₂" wide
Mojave Desert, California

Intriguing because of its multilayered shelters, two near the top and one running the full length of the stone at the bottom, this suiseki shows how desert stones can provide intricately detailed shapes that still fit the classical description.   Photo by Marge Blasingame

Sheet waterfall stone *(Nunodaki-ishi)*
6" tall and 5" wide
Canada

A treasured gift from the late Nadine Biel, this excellent suiseki shows a type of waterfall often called a "sheet waterfall" because of its broad white water. The dai was carved by Ned Tucker.

Animal-shaped stone *(Dobutsu-seki)*
3" tall and 3" wide
Mojave Desert, California

This is an object stone whose shape is open to viewer interpretation. At the top of the pedestal, my daughter sees a monster on the run. I see it as a shelter stone (Yadori-ishi). What do you see?

Thatched hut stone *(Kuzuya-ishi)*
2¹/₂" tall and 3" wide
Japan

This classically shaped hut stone has been enhanced to accentuate its features. It is an excellent accent piece when displayed with a bonsai, as on page 36.

Fish-shaped stone *(Uogata-ishi)*
2" tall and 4" wide
China

This orca whale appears to be jumping out of the water. The suiban with sand helps carry that idea.

Boat-shaped stone *(Funagata-ishi)*
1¹/₂" tall and 4¹/₂" wide
California desert

This suiseki could be a tugboat or a submarine. It would also display well in a suiban with sand to indicate water.

Distant mountain stone *(Toyama-ishi)*
2³/₄" tall and 4" wide
California desert

The soft, rounded shoulders and top of this stone suggest a distant mountain. Or perhaps you see a coastal rock stone (Iwagata-ishi).

Photo by Marge Blasingame

Puddle stone *(Mizutamari-ishi)*
1" tall and 4" wide
Rogue River, California

Rich black, with three distinct depressions that hold water, this suiseki gives the feel of low hills with lakes and ponds.

Mountain stone *(Yamagata-ishi)*
5" tall and 8¹/₂" wide
Russian River, California

The fine white sand represents snow around the base of this snow-capped mountain, displayed in a suiban twice its length. This viewing stone was a gift to me from Harry Hirao.

Waterfall stone *(Taki-ishi)*
5" tall and 9" wide
Northern California dry riverbed

A dramatic waterfall stone with multiple cascades, this viewing stone emphasizes through its stark black and whites the strength of mountains and their spectacular scenes.

Coastal rock stone *(Iwagata-ishi)*
3" tall and 4" wide
California desert

Hewn by fierce winds and the driving waves that crash against its shore, this coastal rock endures the elements.

Shelter stone *(Yadori-ishi)*
3¹/₂" tall and 2¹/₂" wide
Mojave Desert, California

The large overhanging top creates a shelter above the ledge at the bottom. Smaller shelters partway up add interest. Set in its dai without cutting, it makes a fine suiseki.

Scenic landscape stone *(Sansui kei-seki)*
(Desert monument stone)
Mojave Desert, California
  and
Desert barberry *(Mahonia sp.)*
Northern Arizona

This display reverses the role of stones and trees. The suiseki is nine inches tall and the Mahonia, two inches. The monuments depicted by the stone in this desert scene are made to seem larger by the small accent plant. An unusual stone, this is actually two monuments side by side. At one angle of display they seem as one stone, but slightly turned, the deep chasm dividing them is apparent.

Hinoki cypress *(Chamaecyparis obtusa nana)*
  and
Thatched hut stone *(Kuzuya-ishi)*

Here we see how a bonsai can be displayed using suiseki as an accent. The tree is twenty-seven inches tall and the stone two and one half inches, emphasizing the idea of a small hut under a large tree. This tree has been in training in my collection for thirty years. See page 31 for details on the stone.

Appendix

Stone Classifications

English term	Japanese Term
Abstract-pattern stone	*Chusho-seki*
Pit-mark-pattern stone	*Sudachi-ishi*
Snake-pattern stone	*Jagure-ishi*
Tangled-net-pattern stone	*Itomaki-ishi*
Tiger-stripe-pattern stone	*Tora-ishi*
▪	
Black stone	*Kuro-ishi*
Beautiful stone	*Biseki*
▪	
Cape stone	*Misaki-ishi*
Cave stone	*Dokutsu-ishi*
Celestial-pattern stone	*Gensho-seki*
Moon-pattern stone	*Tsukigata-ishi*
Star-pattern stone	*Hoshigata-ishi*
Sun-pattern stone	*Higata-ishi*

Coastal rock stone	*Iwagata-ishi*
■	
Hill or Slope stone	*Doha-ishi*
■	
Island stone	*Shimagata-ishi*
■	
Mountain stone	*Yamagata-ishi*
Distant mountain stone	*Toyama-ishi*
Double-peaked mountain stone	*Soho-seki*
Near-view mountain stone	*Kinzan-seki*
Single-peak mountain stone	*Koho-ishi*
Mountain stream stone	*Keiryu-ishi*
■	
Object stone	*Keisho-seki*
Animal-shaped stone	*Dobutsu-seki*
Bird-shaped stone	*Torigata-ishi*
Boat-shaped stone	*Funagata-ishi*
Bridge-shaped stone	*Hashi-ishi*
Fish-shaped stone	*Uogata-ishi*
Human-shaped stone	*Sugata-ishi*
Insect-shaped stone	*Mushigata-ishi*
Thatched hut stone	*Kuzuya-ishi*
■	
Pattern stone	*Mon'yo-seki*
Plant-pattern stone	*Kigata-ishi*
Chrysanthemum-pattern stone	*Kikumon-seki*
Flower-pattern stone	*Hanagata-ishi*
Fruit-pattern stone	*Migata-ishi*

Grass-pattern stone	*Kusagata-ishi*
Leaf-pattern stone	*Hagata-ishi*
Plum-blossom-pattern stone	*Baika-seki*
Plateau stone	*Dan-ishi*
Pool or Lake stone	*Tamari-ishi*

■

Rocky Bay or Inlet or Coastal stone	*Iwagata-ishi*
Scenic landscape stone	*Sansui kei-seki*
Shelter stone	*Yadori-ishi*
Shore stone	*Isogata-ishi*
Slope stone	*Doha-ishi*
Step stone (multilevel)	*Dan-ishi*

■

Tunnel stone	*Domon-ishi*

■

Waterfall stone	*Taki-ishi*
Dry waterfall stone	*Karedaki-ishi*
Sheet waterfall stone	*Nunodaki-ishi*
Thread waterfall stone	*Itodaki-ishi*
Water pool or puddle stone	*Mizutamari-ishi*
Weather-pattern stone	*Tenko-seki*
Lightning-pattern stone	*Raiko-seki*
Rain-pattern stone	*Amagata-ishi*
Snow-pattern stone	*Yukigata-ishi*

A low range of mountains,
Toward them I am running.
From the top of these mountains
I shall see the dawn.

—TOHONO O'ODHAM